MW00682828

Instant
DOMINICAN
REPUBLIC

APA PUBLICATIONS

Part of the Langenscheidt Publishing Group

L

CONTENTS

Compiled by Lesley Gordon
Photography by Wolfgang Rössig,
 Montreal Expos, Boston Red Sox,
 Tom Conlin/Aquatic Adventures
Cover photograph: Monika Latzel

All Rights Reserved
First Edition 2001

Distributed in the UK & Ireland by
GeoCenter International Ltd
The Viables Centre, Harrow Way
Basingstoke, Hampshire RG22 4BJ
Fax: (44 1256) 817-988

Distributed in the United States by
Langenscheidt Publishers, Inc.
46–35 54th Road, Maspeth, NY 11378
Tel: (718) 784-0055. Fax: (718) 784-0640

Worldwide distribution enquiries:
APA Publications GmbH & Co. Verlag KG
Singapore Branch, Singapore
38 Joo Koon Road, Singapore 628990
Tel: (65) 865-1600. Fax: (65) 861-6438

Printed in Singapore by
Insight Print Services (Pte) Ltd
38 Joo Koon Road, Singapore 628990
Tel: (65) 865-1600. Fax: (65) 861-6438

© *2001 APA Publications GmbH & Co.
Verlag KG, Singapore Branch, Singapore*

www.insightguides.com

A TROPICAL PARADISE

The Dominican Republic evokes images of palm-fringed strips of golden sand, lapped by warm clear waters. Indeed there are many miles of gleaming beaches to enjoy from the Costa Caribe in the southeast to the Costa del Coco in the far east. But scratch the surface of this mountainous land and you will discover that there is so much more to see and experience.

The country known as the Dominican Republic in fact covers about two-thirds of the island of Hispaniola, totalling 48,734 sq. km (18,816 sq. miles), while the Republic of Haiti has the remaining third, approximately 27,750 sq. km (10,714 sq. miles). To the west is Cuba, southwest is Jamaica and east is Puerto Rico and the chain of the Lesser Antilles.

Protected within the country's vast national parks are cascading waterfalls, tumbling rivers and vast forests – the habitats of rich and varied flora and fauna. The wildlife includes some found exclusively on the island in its fertile valleys and dry, arid desert land in the west around Lago Enriquillo.

Hispaniola has a rich and colourful natural environment that is home to more than 5,000 plant species, almost half of which are endemic – from ferns and bamboo to frangipani and hibiscus. Parts of the Dominican Republic's coast contain tangles of thick mangroves: red fresh-

Right: *parading on the Malecón*

water ones can exist in high water, while black mangroves are more comfortable in shallow water and play host to flocks of pelicans, herons and other birdlife that feed off the shellfish, shrimp and small fry living there.

The highest points in the Caribbean are in the Dominican Republic too; a magnet to travellers attracted by the challenge of hiking through the mountain ranges and scaling the peaks, especially the highest elevation in the Antilles, Pico Duarte, in the heart of the Cordillera Central.

In the tranquil northwest of the country – the agricultural Cibao Valley and the verdant hills of the Cordillera Central – country life continues in much the same way as it always has done. Sugar cane and fruit plantations, paddy fields and fragrant alpine forests dominate the landscape, while higher up, the lush, cool hills offer some relief from the tropical temperatures inland.

Above: *pink flamingoes, Parque Zoológico in Santo Domingo*

Colourful Capital

The nation's vibrant capital city, Santo Domingo is rich in the historical monuments of the founding fathers. Beautiful centuries-old architecture stands side by side with modernist-style buildings. The capital is the commercial and cultural centre of the Republic, where the handsome tree-lined boulevards are home to chic boutiques, museums and galleries. And just as in any major city, locals hurry to attend to their everyday business. But typical of the peoples of the Caribbean and Latin America, they find time to stop and chat in the pretty squares and parks.

Elsewhere in the country are such archaeological gems as the ruins of La Isabela in the north between Puerto Plata and Monte Cristi: this was the first permanent settlement in the Americas. There are sandy beaches for relaxation and sunbathing and warm lapping waters for cooling down. All-inclusive hotels jostle for space along the coast from Boca Chica to Punta Cana, the Samaná Peninsula to the Amber Coast. Sosúa and Cabarete on the north coast have some of the best scuba diving and windsurfing.

The infectious rhythms of merengue music, played at ear-splitting volume, can be heard almost everywhere from beach barbecues to the city nightclubs and the funky bars that entertain until daybreak.

Right: swinging in the Parque Zoológico

HISTORICAL HIGHLIGHTS

500 BC Arrival of the pre-Ceramic Ciboney people – fishers and foragers from Mexico and Florida.

AD 650–1200 Taínos, after gradually migrating from what is now Venezuela, reach the Greater Antilles in dug-out canoes, escaping Carib aggressors who follow them up the island chain.

1492 Christopher Columbus establishes the first European settlement in the Americas on the island he calls Hispaniola.

1493 Columbus's second expedition to Hispaniola brings colonists and gold hunters.

1494 Pope Alexander VI approves Treaty of Tordesillas, dividing up the New World between Spain and Portugal.

1496 Columbus's brother, Bartolomé, founds the south coast settlement of Nueva Isabela, later moved and renamed Santo Domingo.

1498 Columbus's third voyage; growing tension in Hispaniola ends in revolt.

1500 The Columbus brothers are shipped back to Spain by the commissioner, Francisco de Bobadilla.

1509–24 Diego Columbus presides as Governor of Hispaniola and Viceroy of the Indies.

1511 Fray Antón de Montesinos criticises the colonists' many abuses of the Taínos' human rights.

Above: Taíno petroglyphs, Museo del Hombre Dominicano

1586 Sir Francis Drake sacks Santo Domingo.

1650s A group of French buccaneers settles in the northwest of the island.

1795 Treaty of Bâle cedes Spanish Santo Domingo on the eastern side of Hispaniola to France.

1809 Eastern part of Hispaniola returns to Spanish control after 14-year French occupation.

1821 Spanish Santo Domingo gains independence, and is named "Spanish Haiti".

1822 Haiti's Jean-Pierre Boyer occupies Santo Domingo.

1823 The US President, James Monroe, proclaims the "Monroe Doctrine", underlining American domination of the Caribbean region.

1838 Founding of the underground *La Trinitaria* movement in Santo Domingo, which pledges to achieve independence from Haiti as the new República Dominicana (Dominican Republic).

1843 Boyer is overthrown.

1844 Independence of the Dominican Republic after Haitian troops are expelled.

1848 Haiti, under Faustin

Above: bust of Columbus, San Cristobal

Soulouque, attempts to invade the Dominican Republic; a second invasion in 1859 also ends in failure.

1861 Spain re-occupies the Dominican Republic, but it withdraws in 1865 after the "War of Restoration".

1882 Ulises Heureaux begins a 17-year dictatorship in the Dominican Republic.

1905 US takes control of Dominican customs to prevent further interference by European powers.

1914 Opening of the Panama Canal increases the strategic importance of the Caribbean.

1916 US forces take control of the Dominican Republic, a year after occupying Haiti during a period of extreme political instability.

1925 The US withdraws from the Dominican Republic.

1930 Rafael Leonidas Trujillo takes power in the Dominican Republic, starting a 30-year dictatorship.

1935 Trujillo orders the massacre of some 15,000 Haitian migrants in the Dominican Republic.

1939 The founding of the Dominican Revolutionary Party (PRD) by exiled anti-

Trujillo social democrats.

1961 Trujillo is assassinated.

1962 Reformist Juan Bosch of the PRD triumphs in Dominican Republic elections but is overthrown by the military a year later, leading to civil unrest.

1965 US occupation of the Dominican Republic, intended to prevent "another Cuba".

1966 Joaquín Balaguer wins the first of six controversial elections in the Dominican Republic.

1978 The PRD led by Antonio Guzmán, takes power in Dominican Republic after a threatened military coup.

1982 Guzmán commits suicide following a corruption scandal involving members of his family; the PRD party holds on to power with Salvador Jorge Blanco at the helm.

1986 Joaquín Balaguer returns to power. He is re-elected two more times: in 1990 and again in 1994.

1991 Balaguer orders the deportation of all illegal Haitian immigrants under the age of 16 and over the age of 60.

1996 Balaguer is forced to stand down in the Dominican Republic after the disputed elections of 1994, and Leonel Fernández wins what are seen as free and fair elections.

1997 Historic meeting held between Leonel Fernández and René Préval, the Haitian president, raises hopes of better cross-border relations.

1998 The PRD wins in congressional elections.

2000 PRD's Hipólito Mejiá wins the presidential elections in the first round of voting.

Left: fighting the War of Independence ***Above:*** *political graffiti*

PEOPLE AND CULTURE

The official ideology suggests that the Dominican Republic is an Hispanic, Catholic nation, European in composition and Western in outlook. In fact the historical influence of the Spanish and the more recent North American influx has shaped the Dominican Republic and its people.

A Migrant Nation

Although present-day Dominicans may like to romanticise a long-gone indigenous heritage, in reality most of the country's 8 million people are descended from later arrivals, most notably Spanish and Africans, but also other, smaller groups of incomers. The first Spanish settlers were hardly numerous, and many were only too eager to abandon the colony for greener pastures elsewhere.

It was only at the end of the 18th century that the colony's population stabilised, helped by a large influx of immigrants from the Canary Islands. Subsequent European migration came in fits and starts, encouraged by government efforts to "whiten" the population; some Spaniards stayed after the brief recolonisation of 1861–65; a significant Italian community began to arrive from the 1870s onwards; and a small, but conspicuous mix of Europeans settled in the 20th century, some escaping persecution by Nazi Germany.

Above: a friendly welcome

The black population has always been small compared to neighbouring Haiti's, yet despite Dominican delusions of racial superiority, people of African descent have been present in large numbers since the mid-1550s.

By the end of the 18th century, 30 percent of the population officially comprised of slaves, with many more blacks classified as free citizens. The 22-year occupation of the territory by Haiti inevitably added to the black population. More recently, migrant cane-cutters from the smaller English-speaking Caribbean islands of St Kitts, Nevis and Anguilla came in the early 20th century to work on plantations around La Romana.

Outside Influence

Several small migrant communities have made a significant impact on Dominican society. From the late 19th century a substantial group of Syrians and Palestinians, commonly known as *turcos*, established themselves as traders in Santo Domingo

Above: young Dominicans are influenced by American tastes

and the main towns. Mostly Maronite Christians, they rapidly earned a reputation as shrewd business operators.

A Jewish community has also contributed to Dominican life – firstly the Sephardic Jews who settled in the early colonial period, and more recently refugees from Hitler's Germany who put down roots in the northern town of Sosúa.

But perhaps the oddest experiment in immigration policy involved Japanese farmers brought over by President Trujillo in the 1930s to populate the territory adjacent to Haiti. This attempt to create a *cordon sanitaire* around the border failed due to government neglect, and the disgruntled Japanese soon moved on.

Have and Have Nots

A few residential districts of Santo Domingo or Santiago rival the plushest suburbs of Florida or California. TV satellite dishes and swimming pools can be glimpsed behind high walls, while armed guards and trained dogs protect lavish mansions. But just

Above: an architectural remnant in San Pedro Macorís

a few miles away, in areas like La Ciénaga (the Swamp) or Capotillo, are some of the Caribbean's worst shanty towns, where poverty, crime and disease are all too common. Some of these slums cling to the banks of the River Ozama, visible from Santo Domingo's main bridges, and face the constant threat of flood. Tiny huts of wood and corrugated iron are crammed together without sanitary facilities or services of any sort.

Average per capita income in the Republic is about $1,600 per year (compared to under $500 in Haiti), but this average conceals a sharp difference between the wealthy top 10 percent, who account for 40 percent of income, and the bottom 10 percent – who receive less than 2 percent. The rich are a mix of old and new. "Old money" takes the form of ranching, sugar and tobacco interests, controlled by traditional light-skinned families, some of whom can trace their lineage back to the *conquistadores*. "New money" is more likely to derive from tourism, the new

manufacturing sector and the sometimes dubious activities of Dominicans in the United States. Needless to say, the old elite despises the *nouveaux riches*, who are not welcome in traditional upper-class establishments such as the Country Club.

Visa Dreams

Migration provides the slim prospect of upward mobility that is lacking in the Dominican Republic. In his song *Visa para un Sueño* (Visa for a Dream), the Dominican *merengue* singer, Juan

Right: *a country home*

Luis Guerra expresses the fears and yearning felt by so many of his compatriots as they balance separation and homesickness against the hope for a better life.

The reality of life in the US often fails to match up to the dream, but North American culture continues to exert a strong fascination for many Dominicans, especially the young. Older Dominicans may remember the humiliations of the 1965 occupation, when US Marines searched passers-by at checkpoints, but younger generations are attracted by the fast lifestyle that they see daily on satellite TV. As more and more Dominicans experience life in the US, so American tastes and habits become increasingly commonplace.

But the Dominican Republic is not yet entirely Americanised. While baseball and Coca-Cola are almost ubiquitous, the popularity of rum and cock-fighting points to another cultural dimension, both Hispanic and Caribbean.

Acts of Faith

Every year on 21 January thousands of pilgrims make their

way to the vast modern cathedral in the eastern city of Higüey to pay tribute to Our Lady of Altagracia, patron of the Republic since 1922 and reputed to perform healing miracles. It is one of the strongest manifestations of religious faith in a society that claims to be 90 percent Catholic. While Catholicism is an important element in Dominican cultural identity, in reality the Church is politically weak, conservative and in desperate need

of priests and money. As elsewhere in the region, Protestant churches are making gradual in-roads and competing with traditional Catholicism, but the Church still has influence in education and social welfare. In some of the most deprived areas, priests have also been at the forefront of organising community self-help groups.

Ubiquitous Sounds

The manic mayhem of *merengue*, the Dominican national music, is a serious contender for the fastest music in the Caribbean and it can be heard all over the country – in the streets, restaurants, bars and even taxis – mostly played at full volume.

The origins of *merengue* are undocumented. One theory suggests that the original dance was based on the popular *upa* from Cuba, which travelled to Puerto Rico where it was banned as immoral in 1848. After adapting steps from the *contradanza*, it was then referred to as the *merengue*. An account of its first performance in the Dominican Republic goes back to the 1844

Left and Above: the new and the old cathedrals in Higüey

war against the Haitians, when the victorious Dominicans sang and danced a song about a deserter: *Toma' Juyo con la Bandera* (Thomas Fled with the Flag).

Despite its obscure beginnings, *merengue* developed from folk forms before going on to establish itself not only as the national dance music but as an international genre, which even eclipsed *salsa* as *the* Latin dance sound of the 1980s. Of the many Creolised European dance forms to originate from the Caribbean, *merengue* has probably travelled the furthest and certainly moves the fastest.

What began as a very restrained European dance soon took on the Afro-Caribbean features of vibrant rhythms and the call-and-response final section of the accompanying songs, with their wide-ranging topics. Predictably spurned by the white and mulatto elite as being vulgar, *merengue* was enthusiastically embraced by everybody else.

The American occupation of 1916–24 fuelled a nascent

Above: a typical country store and cafe

nationalism and with it bourgeois acceptance of the *merengue*. It was elevated to the status of national music and dance by a 1936 decree. Urban dance bands were legally required to incorporate *merengue* in their swing band repertoires. These bands, heavily influenced by Cuban *mambo*, added the exhilarating trumpet and sax arrangements that still feature in contemporary *merengue*.

Dominican Cuisine

Dining at a Dominican home involves being treated to one of several favourite platters. Stories of *merengue*, politics and national pride will be nourished by *la bandera Dominicana* – "flying the flag" at dinner refers to the national dish of rice, beans, chicken or meat, with avocado, plantain, yucca and salad: food that is tasty, wholesome and heavy. Rice and beans, *arroz con habichuelas*, form the foundation of most meals – good news for vegetarians. However, chicken, chicken and chicken is the other staple ingredient. No self-respecting restaurant leaves *arroz con pollo* (chicken and rice) off the menu.

Much of Dominican culinary life occurs on the street. Fried foods are readily served up from mobile vans. A sampling of *yanniqueques* (Johnny cakes), *pastelitos* (meat or cheese-filled pastry turnovers) and *quipes* (ground beef encased in cracked wheat) provide a good entrée. *Chimichurris* are more substantial pork sandwiches off the spit.

Right: fried fish and plantain

Bars and Cafes

Cafe society has found its tropical home in the Dominican Republic. Cafes cater for all tastes – coffee-fuelled morning reviews of the newspapers, sober afternoons of delicious ice creams and outrageously divine fruitshakes, or rum-soaked cocktail evenings. *Batidas con leche*, a rich mixture of condensed milk, sugar, crushed ice and a bewildering range of fruits will keep you nourished until supper. *Lechosa* (papaya), *zapote* and the unusually named orange-based *morir soñando* ("to die dreaming") are particular favourites.

If fruit juice alone suffices, then *jugos* will be the order of the day. You may wish to ask the waiter to go easy on the sugar, or leave it out all together. *Jugo de china* and *chinola* – orange and passion fruit – frequently top the taste polls.

Rum is sold in three general categories – *blanco*, *dorado*, and *añejo*. The former, lighter, rums are used in cocktails and with mixers. The darker blends are more suited to less vigorous adulteration. True *añejos* are best taken neat. *Un servicio* consists of a bottle of rum, a bucket of ice and *refrescos* (soft drinks) as mixers. Given the strength, quality and abundance of Domini-

can rums, the ability to hide alcohol within sweet fruit flavours, as exemplified by the ubiquitous *ron ponch*, is a dangerous trait among Dominican bartenders. Many a happy hour at sunset can slip smoothly through to a melancholic dawn.

The Big Hitters

There is one great passion that runs through all classes of Dominican society, and that is baseball. This is a game in which two teams of nine players each try to win points by hitting a small ball so hard with a bat that the one or more runners spread out across the field – in a diamond

marked by white cushions – can manage to run to safety before the opposing team recovers the ball. The movements on the field will long remain a mystery to the uninitiated spectator, but the Dominicans, just like the North Americans, love the game.

Baseball remains without doubt the nation's favourite sport. Six teams compete for the national championship: two each from the Cibao Valley and Santo Domingo and one each from La Romana and San Pedro de Macorís. They compete six days a week, and the main season runs from October to January.

No other Central or South American country can claim as many top-rate players in the US as the little half-island in the Caribbean. More than 50 Dominicans currently take to the field for the Major League teams, and another 500 or so play for the Minors.

Left: bars proliferate *Above: Boston Red Sox star Pedro Martínez*

AN AMERICAN IMPORT

In the early part of the 20th century, from 1916 to 1924, US troops occupied the Dominican Republic for the first time, in support of the Monroe Doctrine. The "Americanos" brought their favourite game with them to the island – baseball. It wasn't long before the young islanders had formed a team that was good enough to take on the international competition. During the 1950s the first Dominicans successfully played the game in the Major League of the United States. The Alou brothers and Juan Marischal are famous names to this day.

The Dominican Republic has now become a paradise for talent scouts working on behalf of the Major League clubs. Every winter, American scouts occupy the stands of the island's baseball stadiums on the lookout for future home-run record-breakers. The Los Angeles Dodgers, Cleveland Indians, Chicago Cubs, Boston Red Sox and other clubs run training camps in many loca-

tions throughout the Dominican Republic. In some of them, the young hopefuls undergo intensive training for three months without a break, while other US clubs send coaches into schools every day, where they spend their afternoons teaching boys how they can best hit the ball into the invisible strike zone.

A large number of the players who have made it to the top in the United States grew up in the *bateyes*, the impoverished barrack-like settlements

Left: *Vlademir Guerrero,* beisbol *hero*

around San Pedro de Macorís where the sugar-cane workers live. Sammy Sosa, Pedro Martínez, Raúl Mondesí, José Martínez, Tony Peña, Tony Fernandez and Manny Ramirez are all top stars in the baseball firmament of the US. The legendary Matty Alou once joked about the remarkable success of the Dominicans: "It must be the water".

Fun Outdoors

The Dominican Republic is home to the Antilles' highest mountain, Pico Duarte – at 3,087 metres (10,128 ft), a hiker's favourite – while the north coast is one of the world's major whale-spotting and windsurfing destinations.

There is a well-developed eco and adventure tourism infrastructure with activities ranging from hiking and diving to kayaking, rafting, tubing, climbing, abseiling, caving, canyoning, cascading, paragliding, mountain biking and horse riding.

Above: beach life in Boca Chica

DIVE DOMINICANA

Divers, windsurfers, mountain bikers and horse riders, among others, head northwards: Cabarete is classed as one of the best windsurfing beaches, and hosts World Cup competitions. A protective reef and varying wind conditions make it ideal for both beginners and world-class windsurfers. Neighbouring Sosua, with its shallow reefs, has the best diving for beginners, but there are also sites for the more advanced, such as Las Palmitas, the Airport Wall and the interconnecting tunnels of La Piramide.

In the south, close to Santo Domingo, La Caleta National Underwater Park has reef and wreck dives, as well as freshwater cave diving. Saona Island is a good site for spotting big fish and Punta Cana on the east coast has the Dominican Republic's longest coral reef, nearly 30 km (19 miles), which is protected by an active preservation programme.

IN THE MOUNTAINS

On the north coast and the northern mountain range there are mountain bike trails ranging from easy to advanced off-road or single-track mountain passages. Those who prefer to tackle mountains on foot can try the strenuous hike up Pico Duarte

Above: letting the mule take the strain in Monte Cristi

(or cheat by riding a mule) and the easier climbs up Pico Yaque or Mt Isabel de Torres in Puerto Plata.

If you want to get wet, try rubber rafting on the Río Yaque del Norte in Jarabacoa. You can go solo without a paddle in an oversized rubber tube on the same river, or the Río Jamao al Norte or Río Isabela in Santo Domingo.

For the truly adventurous there's cascading and canyoning. Cascading involves climbing to the top of a waterfall and then abseiling down the middle of the cascade to the bottom, where you jump into the water. The best cascading sites are El Salto del Jimenoa, Cascada del Limón, Cascada Ojo de Agua and El Salto de Baiguate. Canyoning takes you up the wall of a river gorge with rope and harness. When you're high enough you jump into the river. The best sites are in La Damajagua in Imbert and the Jaraba-coa area. You can paraglide over mountains and rivers from any convenient ridge, given the appropriate wind conditions.

Wildlife

Flora and fauna are abundant with over 5,600 plant species (including more than 300 endemic orchids); 258 bird species (including the Hispaniolan parrot and parakeet); four species of sea turtles and two freshwater species; reptiles such as the American crocodiles of Lago

Right: the stork is one of 258 bird species on the island

Enriquillo and the rhinoceros iguana; 33 land mammals (among which are the endangered solenodonte and jutia), as well as the endangered Antillean manatee and the humpback whale.

With 16 national parks, six scientific reserves, natural monuments, protected areas (islands, bays, river estuaries, lagoons) and ecological corridors, the Dominican government is taking a systematic approach to preserving the environment. Construction is forbidden in the 67 protected areas. Establishing the central parks of Armando Bermudez and José del Carmen Ramirez has saved the last extensive areas of forest, and the Plan Sierra reforestation project is on stream at nearby San José de las Matas.

WHALE-WATCHING

Several thousand North Atlantic humpback whales converge on the Banco de la Plata (Silver Bank) 140 km (87 miles) off the north coast during the breeding season from December to March. The Silver Bank is the most important humpback sanctuary in the Atlantic, with up to 3,000 whales visiting annually.

These migratory animals are cetaceans: marine mammals that are warm-blooded, give birth to suckling young and breathe air. They communicate with one another using a song-like call, and males compete in loud groups for the right to mate.

From January to March there are day trips from Puerto Plata out to the

Left: a breathtaking humpback whale

warm waters around the Banco de la Plata, which lies within the Silver Bank Marine Sanctuary, about 100 km (60 miles) north of Puerto Plata. Visitors can also observe humpback and pilot whales, bottlenose, spinner and spotted dolphin off Bahía de Samaná (Samaná Bay) in the northeast. Both places offer breathtaking sights of migrating humpback whales.

With powerful binoculars the whales' mating rituals and calving can be seen from dry land at Bahía de Samaná, but it is nothing like the view from a whale-watching boat. One can witness fantastic visual displays because much of the activity is played out on the surface of the water.

Though access to the protected area is restricted, tours can sometimes include an opportunity for the brave to float in the ocean alongside the magnificent creatures in what is known as a soft-in-water encounter.

www.oceanic-society.org

Above: *a turtle in Acuario Nacional, Santo Domingo*

AN A–Z OF TOP SIGHTS

SANTO DOMINGO

More than 2 million Dominicans live in the sprawling metropolis and bustling hubbub of the nation's capital. At any one time, the bulk of residents seem to be out and about – negotiating cracked pavements or gushing along the arterial roads that criss-cross the city and lend a semblance of order to the urban bustle.

Acuario Nacional

Located a few blocks to the south of the Parque Mirador del Este on the Avenida España, the aquarium is well worth an extended trip. The star of the show is Tamaury, an orphaned manatee rescued off the southwest coast of the island. An underwater walkway allows visitors to watch the sharks playing overhead, while a host of fish swim alongside in the massive transparent tank.

Altar de la Patria

Built in 1976, the mausoleum houses three white marble statues and the remains of the statesmen who engineered the fledgling republic during the 19th century: Francisco del Rosario Sánchez, Juan Pablo Duarte and Ramón Matías Mella. Stern-looking military sentries guard the monolithic solemnity of the site.

Ciudad Universitaria

The lively thoroughfare of Calle Santiago leads to the Ciudad Universitaria, home to one of the oldest universities in the Americas. It may lack funds and architectural longevity, although orig-

Left: *a soldier guards the Altar de la Patria*

inally founded in 1538, but the Autonomous University of Santo Domingo (UASD) makes up for material shortfall with a proud reputation and a history of vigorous student activism that consistently challenges the political and social inequalities evident in Dominican society. A range of concerts, films, theatre productions – and demonstrations – are regularly held on site.

Faro a Colón

Dreamed up in the 1920s to honour the *conquistador*'s arrival in the Americas, original plans for Columbus' lighthouse were penned by British architect, J.L. Greave. Funding and interest languished for almost six decades, until the idea was resurrected in order to commemorate the 500th anniversary of Columbus' landfall in 1992. The lighthouse is an 800-metre (875-yard) long concrete edifice, shaped as a recumbent cross, which projects a laser image of the crucifix into the heavens – when funds allow. At the centre, the tomb of Columbus is under military guard. Reproductions of documents and colonial artefacts and exhibitions from other countries highlight the path of the Conquest.

Jardín Botánico Nacional

The Jardín Botánico Nacional on Avenida República de Colombia is fair reward for journeying to the northwestern edge of the city. In the residential suburb of Arroyo Hondo, the botanical gardens cover 180 hectares (450 acres) and exhibit a variety of tropical and aquatic plants, ferns, a herbarium and 200 species of palm. A pavilion houses the famous collection of over 300 indigenous orchid varieties.

The Malecón

Avenida George Washington (known as the Malecón), which skirts the seafront from the port, is a welcome escape from the buzzing throng of shoppers. Gingerbread lattices lace their way through tumbling balconies. Approaching the sea, the imposing statue of the indigenous people's rights petitioner, Fray Antón de Montesinos, looms to the left, overlooking the harbour entrance and marking the head of the Malecón.

The relative inactivity of the afternoon rolls over to the dusk arrival of the jogging set, to be replaced by a busy nightlife clientele. Roadside bars spring up and *merengue* blasts forth at the weekend. The volume increases impressively for the annual *merengue* festival during the last week of July and first week of August. Carnaval, at the end of February, is another occasion for a boisterous seafront gathering.

*Left: Faro a Colón **Above:** at the seafront on the Malecón*

The Mercado Modelo

This busy covered craft market focuses largely on the tourist trade, but it is also used by locals. A plethora of stallholders eagerly divert passers-by, proffering woodcarvings, paintings, T-shirts, amber jewellery, dolls, ornaments, ironwork… a veritable lion's den, treasure trove and old curiosity shop combined. Be prepared to bargain, be seduced and leave with a purchase.

Palacio Nacional

Headquartered in a pink, domed baroque fantasy at the intersection of avenidas Doctor Delgado and México, the Palacio Nacional combines neoclassical style, presidential grandeur, regal decadence and keen security. It was designed by Italian architect Guido d'Alessandro during the late 1940s to match the magnificence of the dictatorship, and Trujillo's troubled ghost allegedly whisks through the ornately mirrored and heavily furnished salons, haunting present incumbents.

Parque Mirador del Sur

Bordered to the north by affluent suburbs and adjacent to the foreign diplomatic missions dotted along Avenida Anacaona, the Parque Mirador del Sur is a popular location for in-line skaters, cyclists, runners, and people out for a stroll. The 7-km (5-mile) stretch of paths and lawns is a much appreciated retreat away from rush-hour traffic fumes. Police close the through road to

Above: Palacio Nacional

vehicles during morning and evening peak hours. The park lies along a limestone ridge that hides a series of caves: the Cueva del Paseo de los Indios has a notable bat population, but perhaps the best-known cave is the Guácara Taína on Avenida Mirador del Sur. Converted into a lively subterranean music venue, this is where *capitaleños* make merry until dawn at the weekends.

Parque Zoológico

Along Avenida los Reyes Católicos, the Parque Zoológico is an undervalued and undervisited nugget in the northwest of the city. Enhanced by its relative isolation, the 160 hectares (400 acres) of landscaped gardens and sensitively housed animal inmates provide an unexpected attraction. Pink flamingos stand on sentry duty around the lagoon, while tigers stalk relatively open enclosures. Rare Dominican fauna, the hutía and solenodon, find refuge here.

Plaza de la Cultura

Just a few blocks to the north on Avenida Máximo Gómez, the Plaza de la Cultura provides a feast of opportunities to satiate the cultural appetite. Set amid pleasant lawns and landscaped gardens, the modernist complex houses the most important arts institutions in the country.

The Teatro Nacional is the imposing home of classical arts in the Dominican Republic. Standards are high: national and international artists perform ballet, opera and orchestral concerts here regularly.

Right: a train shuttle for tourists

The Museo de Arte Moderno houses an excellent exposition of contemporary Dominican art. Representations of country life, evolving from the 1930s *costumbrismo* movement, provide a feel for the rural traditions that infuse long-standing notions of *dominicanidad*, which can seldom be experienced during a short stay in the country.

The Museo del Hombre Dominicano has fascinating exhibits of pre-Columbian artefacts and illustrates the history of the Conquest and slavery, demography, folklore, rural life and religious beliefs. The Carnaval display includes brightly coloured masks and garish costumes, and offers a taste of the festive atmosphere.

The Museo Nacional de Historia y Geografía constructs a loose chronological journey around 19th-century Haitian-Dominican tussles, with the assorted memorabilia and personal effects from the two longest-lasting dictatorships.

The Museo Nacional de Historia Natural similarly hawks a lacklustre display of gems, rocks, basic ecology lessons and a stuffy array of taxidermists' treats. Additional enlightenment is restricted to those who are able to understand the Spanish display notes.

Los Tres Ojos

The three sinkhole caves called Los Tres Ojos, "The Three Eyes", are a popular stop, flanked to the north by the Autopista de las Américas. Savour the beauty of the underground caves and the three deep lagoons. Roughly hewn steps lead down to these karst sinkholes, adorned by stalagmites and stalactites.

Left: outside Museo del Hombre Dominicano

ZONA COLONIAL (THE OLD CITY)

At the mouth of the Río Ozama, the Zona Colonial peacefully reflects its important historic past behind ancient thickset walls, which enclose the area within Santo Domingo.

Alcázar de Colón

The Alcázar de Colón is the most spectacular colonial site in the city. This was the palace of Christopher Columbus's son, Diego, who succeeded Ovando as governor of Hispaniola in 1509. After that the Moorish villa was the home of the Spanish Court for more than 60 years and it is where Pizarro, Cortez, Ponce de León and Balboa charted their future conquests.

The coral-stone palace's graceful arched facade is magnificent, and each room has been carefully refurbished with period furniture and paintings donated by the University of Madrid. The palace houses the Museo Virreinal (Viceregal Museum), which

Above: Santo Domingo has attractive parks

displays items of the colonial period. From the second floor there is a grand view of the river and the entire Zona Colonial.

Catedral de Santa María la Menor

Built between 1514 and 1544, Santa María la Menor is believed to be the first cathedral in the Americas. From the outside, the grey limestone cathedral is a majestic sight with massive gates that were originally carved with sculptures of the apostles. When Sir Francis Drake attacked the city in 1586, these were destroyed – as was much else in the building he used as his headquarters – and it wasn't until 1990 that they were replaced with sculptures representing indigenous people.

Inside, the newly restored cathedral is a dizzying mixture of Gothic, Spanish Renaissance and baroque architecture that's surprisingly harmonious. The beautiful stained glass windows have

Above: *the spectacular palace of Alcázar de Colón*

been recreated by the contemporary Dominican artist, Rincón Mora, and other treasures include the 18th-century carved mahogany altar, the silver carillon created by Italian sculptor Benvenuto Cellini (1500–71) and the oil painting by the 17th-century Spanish artist, Bartolomé Murillo.

Convento de los Domínicos

The majestic Convento de los Domínicos stands at the corner of Calle Padre Billini and Calle Duarte Macorís. Founded in 1510, it was visited by Pope Paul III in 1538, and, impressed by the theology lectures that he heard here, he granted it the title of university, making it the oldest university in the New World. Its unusual ceiling depicts both the classical gods and the Christian saints in a single pantheon. The Sun represents God while Mars, Mercury, Jupiter and Saturn are the four evangelists.

Museo de las Atarazanas Reales

La Atarazana (the Royal Mooring Docks) was once the colonial commercial district and it was here naval supplies used to be stored. Today, the small white houses lining the street are home to craft shops, art galleries and restaurants, providing the ideal spot for rest and refreshment.

A little way north along La Ataranza stands the 17th-century Atarazanas Gate and the Museo de las Atarazanas Reales. This maritime museum tells the story of the most famous shipwrecks

Right: Convento de los Domínicos

around the Dominican coast, along with some marvellous exhibits of recovered treasure such as silver and gold coins, porcelain, antique bottles and all manner of interesting contraband. History is graphically captured here.

Museo de las Casas Reales

A fascinating treasure chest of eclectic, colonial objects fill the Museo de las Casas Reales across Calle las Mercedes on the other side of the Panteón. In two 16th-century Renaissance-style mansions, the museum was where the Royal Court or Real Audiencia for the colony sat. On display are antique coins (pieces of eight) and dolls, coats of armour, coaches, treasure from ship-wrecks, gilded Spanish colonial furniture, an apothecary shop and Taíno Indian artefacts. In the cartography room, an enormous map marks the voyages of Columbus. The museum also puts on exhibitions of contemporary Dominican art.

Above: *Museo de las Casas Reales*

Museo de Juan Pablo Duarte

One of the Dominican Republic's founders was born in 1813 at the house that now contains a museum in his honour. The national hero, Juan Pablo Duarte, liberated the Dominican Republic from Haitian domination in 1844, only to see it come under Spanish rule again in 1861. Location: 308 Calle Isabela La Católica.

Panteón Nacional

The neoclassical grey limestone facade of the Panteón Nacional is an unmissable landmark on Calle Las Damas. Constructed between 1714 and 1745 as a Jesuit monastery, the building was given to the Spanish Crown in 1767 when the Jesuits were expelled from Hispaniola and it has served as a tobacco warehouse and a theatre since. In 1955, the dictator Rafael Leonidas Trujillo mandated that the building be transformed into a memorial to the country's national heroes, thinking that he himself would one day be interred here.

Ironically, it now contains the remains of the martyrs who assassinated him: on the ceiling above the altar a commemorative scene of the killing is depicted. Note the exquisite copper chandeliers, a gift from Spain's own dictator, General Franco.

Right: *high art at the Panteón Nacional*

ALONG THE COAST AND ON THE BEACHES

It is a mistake to categorise the eastern part of the country as mainly a "mecca for charter tourists". True, the endless white sand beaches of the Costa Caribe in the southeast and Costa del Coco in the far east are skirted by hundreds of hotels but the interior, especially in the provinces of San Pedro de Macorís, Hato Mayor and La Romana, is still dominated by rural simplicity, where peasants drive their cattle alongside fields of waving sugar cane.

Altos de Chavón

Sitting on a plateau in a spectacular position is the international artists' village of Altos de Chavón. Spoilt Europeans used to sympathetic architecture might trash this mock-Andalusian settlement, yet, undeniably, the beauty of the picturesque limestone buildings and panoramic view over the Río Chavón has to be an inspiration to all. Part of this US$40 million project,

Above: Altos de Chavón

created in the mid-1980s, is the Museo Arqueológico Regional, which houses an extensive collection of Taíno artefacts.

Boca Chica

Boca Chica offers all the hustle and bustle a fun-hungry person could desire. At the weekend, when city dwellers join foreign visitors and descend into the "world's largest bathtub", the reef-protected Playa Boca Chica resembles one crazy MTV-style beach party. Panhandlers offer everything from manicures to fake amber jewellery to hair-braiding.

La Caleta

The small beach at La Caleta is where the Parque Nacional Submarino lies beneath the waves. Here is an intact reef teeming with exotic fish and colourful corals, and three wrecks at this popular spot provide a fascinating day's diving.

Casa de Campo

One of the most sumptuous resorts in the Caribbean, the complex spans over 30 sq km (12 sq miles) with more than 950 palatial villas and smart *casitas* (cabins). The Dominican-born couturier Oscar de la Renta designed the interiors. Oiling this leisure machine are three golf courses, a marina, a polo club, swimming pools, tennis courts, a riding stable and dozens of private beaches. Location: 10 km (6 miles) along the coast, east of La Romana.

Right: Boca Chica

Costa del Coco

Sixty-km (37-mile) long Costa del Coco has the most stunning beaches in the country. Thanks to the coral reefs that protect the bays from the might of the Atlantic, conditions are ideal for swimming, with bathtub temperatures (77°F/25°C), and the forests of coconut palms behind giving the desired shade.

Isla Saona

Robinson Crusoesque Isla Saona lies off the southern tip of the Republic. Part of the Parque Nacional del Este and fringed by virginal, coral sand beaches, the mangrove-lined lagoons of the beautiful 117-sq km (45-sq mile) island are home to endangered birds such as the Hispaniolan lizard cuckoo and zillions of mosquitos.

Manatí Park Bávaro

The Manatí Park Bávaro on Plaza Bávaro is popular with visitors to the Costa del Coco, being the only attraction in the area. The zoo here houses almost every indigenous animal of the republic:

flamingos, manatees, rare birds and spiders, crocodiles and performing parrots. For an additional fee, you can swim with the dolphins.

Punta Cana

Punta Cana and it's beach, the idyllic Playa Punta Cana, lie east of Higüey on the Costa del Coco. The beach stretches for over 2 km (1 mile) and, apart from two all-inclusive resorts and a luxury villa, the tourism magnates have so far kept their hands off it. The lesser-known Playa Juanillo further south is a meeting point for the local youth.

La Romana

La Romana is the financial capital of the southeast, a friendly little town, where visitors can hang out in appealing Euro-style cafes or shop at the Mercado Municipal for souvenirs and fresh herbs. Colourful gingerbread houses front the Avenida Libertad and in the centre is the large, open Parque Central.

San Pedro de Macorís

San Pedro is still synonymous with sugar cane, yet the real money comes from the baseball team Estrellas Orientales and their permanently sold-out stadium Tetelo Vargas. Sammy Sosa, one of North America's *beisbol* heroes, is one of many players exported from the San Pedro team.

Left: Victorian veranda, La Romana **Above:** *in San Pedro de Macorís*

The port town was named for the Macorís Indians, and was founded in 1822, and over the decades has grown into a prosperous centre for the sugar processing industry. It's worth having a look at the neo-Gothic church of San Pedro de Apóstol (1913) on the river bank, and the San Pedro fire station and mansions near Parque Duarte.

THE AMBER COAST

The northeastern region is every bit as varied as its topography – fertile valleys with forested mountains soaring to breathtaking vistas, and 120 km (75 miles) of dazzling beaches. Known as the Amber Coast because of its extensive deposits of the ancient resin, the area's amber is among the most desirable in the world. The north coast has the Atlantic for its front door and a chain of majestic mountains as its backyard, interspersed with beautiful beaches. With a felicitous natural environment, the north coast offers a range of active and high-adventure sports.

Above: Cabarete is good for windsurfing

Cabarete

Cabarete is one of the Caribbean's (and the world's) premier wind-surfing locations. Trade winds here produce the tremendous waves that attract the sport's best amateur surfers from around the globe for the annual Cabarete Race Week in June. Some of the greatest windsurfing is at Playa Encuentro, west of town. In addition to sites for advanced scuba divers, other active sports include tennis, body boarding, horse riding and mountain biking. With its national parks, mountains perfect for hiking, 15 km (9 miles) of beaches and sheltered sandy bays Cabarete and its neighbours are a hub of activity during the holiday season.

Columbus Aquapark

East of Puerto Plata, Columbus Aquapark beckons children of all ages. There are five Olympic-size swimming pools and a diving tower, a slow-flowing "river", water slides, volleyball courts and places to eat. The park is popular with local families.

Fortaleza de San Felipe

At the end of Avenida General Gregorio Luperón (part of the promenade) is what is believed to be the oldest fort in the New World. It was built between 1564 and 1577 on Bahía de Puerto Plata as a northern defence against invasion by sea.

In recent history the fortress has been a prison during the Trujillo years and home to the Brugal rum factory. Today

Right: Fortaleza de San Felipe

it is a museum with a historical photographic exhibition and a display of guns and canon used in independence battles.

Laguna Gri Gri

The cool mangrove-shielded Laguna Gri Gri is where visitors can explore a series of mysterious marine caverns during a leisurely 2-hour boat trip. The caverns were formed by the erosion of soft karst layers and the largest one contains striking stalagmites and stalactites. Scuba diving offshore is excellent.

Museo del Ambar Dominicano

The close proximity of the world's richest deposits of amber, believed to be up to 25 million years old, make the mountains around Puerto Plata the ideal home for the Museo del Ambar Dominicano, a private museum in a beautiful Victorian mansion. The first floor is one of the best places to buy amber with con-

Above: Laguna Gri Gri

fidence, while exhibits on the second floor include extensive examples of the most prized prehistoric animal and plant specimens encased in honey-coloured resins.

Parque Nacional Cabo Francés Viejo

Along the coast towards Cabrera lies the Parque Nacional Cabo Francés Viejo, which preserves precious rainforest with a variety of flora and fauna. The area has extensive freshwater caves where advanced scuba divers with proper training can dive through the wide tunnels. At Cabrera, in the province of María Trinidad Sánchez, is Cuevas de Lago Azul, three beautiful lagoons that flow underground to the sea.

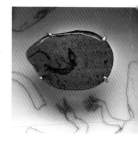

Parque Independencia and La Glorieta

In the centre of Puerto Plata, the beautifully restored Art Deco Catedral San Felipe Apóstol on Calle José del Carmen Ariza stands opposite Parque Independencia – known locally as Parque Central – a pretty park bounded by Calles Beller and Duarte. At the centre of the park is an attractive two-storey Victorian-style wooden structure called La Glorieta.

Pico Isabel de Torres

Pico Isabel de Torres towers 850 metres (2,800 ft) above Puerto Plata and the Parque Nacional Pico Isabel de Torres. Known locally as Loma Isabel de Torres, the peak can be reached by the *teleférico* (cable car). For a small fee the cable car carries

Above: amber on display at the Museo del Ambar Dominicano

visitors from the city to the extensive Botanical Gardens, providing a spectacular view of Puerto Plata Bay below.

Playa Dorada

A private gated resort complex Playa Dorada is around 5 km (3 miles) east of Puerto Plata. It consists of 14 large oceanside all-inclusive hotels sharing a substantial strip of sandy beach, featuring casinos, discos, restaurants and bars, a shopping plaza, swimming pools, a championship 18-hole golf course and a wide variety of sports facilities available to hotel guests only.

Puerto Plata

Founded in 1502, Puerto Plata is the largest city on the Atlantic coast and a focal point of the north. It is steeped in history dating from the arrival of the *conquistadores* to the harsh Trujillo years and beyond. A number of restaurants and hotels line the lively promenade *(malecón)*, which extends about 6 km (4 miles) along the waterfront from Fortaleza de San Felipe at the tip of the penin-

Above: *view of Pico Isabel de Torres, near Puerto Plata*

sula, past the downtown area as far as Long Beach at the eastern end (Avenida Circunvalación Norte). The *malecón* is the venue of some of the city's biggest annual events including Carnival (February or March) and the Merengue Festival in October.

Sosúa

A hotel-laden but relaxed tourist mecca, the beach at Sosúa is lined with bars, restaurants, cafes and souvenir shops. Popular activities include sailing, scuba diving, and snorkelling around the coral reefs just offshore.

The Jewish community in El Batey maintain a one-room Sinagoga de la Comunidad Judía de Sosúa (synagogue) on Calle Dr Alejo Martínez near Calle Dr Rosen. Next door the small Museo de la Comunidad Judía de Sosúa (Museum of the Jewish Community of Sosúa) chronicles the Jewish sojourn here.

THE NORTHWEST

In between the mountains and the Atlantic coast the rolling landscape provides grazing for cattle and goats alongside fields of tobacco and sugar cane. Protected by wide stretches of coral reef, busy with marine life, the Atlantic coast beaches are mainly grey and gravelly and not up to "paradise" standards, apart from a few in resorts such as Cofresí, where scuba diving, fishing and other watersports are good value. This is the coast where Columbus decided to settle his first group of New World colonists.

Right: a growing family

Arqueológia Parque Nacional Historico La Isabela

Here you can see the foundations of Christopher Columbus's original house, and a cemetery containing both Taíno and Spanish burial chambers. A museum contains some interesting artefacts, believed to have belonged to those early colonists, and provides information about the Taínos in pre-Columbian days, although only in Spanish.

La Isabela

Established by Columbus, the original town of La Isabela was located further along the coast, 12 km (7 miles) west of where Luperón is today. But it was doomed from the start, as the first colonists succumbed to disease or became disillusioned and returned to Spain when no gold could be found. Violence and discord, hurricane and fire all added to the demise of the town and by 1498, the remaining colonists had left to start Santo Domingo.

Above: Arqueológia Parque Nacional Historico La Isabela

Some of the remnants of this short-lived town have been unearthed and preserved in the Arqueología Parque Nacional Historico La Isabela. Here you can see the foundations of Christopher Columbus's original house, and a cemetery containing both Taíno and Spanish burial chambers. The reconstructed Templo de las Americas is on the spot where the first Mass in the New World was celebrated on 6 January 1494. La Isabela is also believed to have had the first City Hall in the Americas (1494).

Monte Cristi

The town of Monte Cristi is the capital of the province of the same name. The landscape is dotted with scrub, cacti and xerophytes due to a combination of low rainfall in the region and scorching temperatures, which can reach 35°C (95°F). Flattening out into the delta of the Yaque del Norte, the only relief to the northwest of town is the peak of El Morro, washed by the sea on one side, and waterways with mangroves on the other.

Founded in 1533, the original village was evacuated in 1606 in order to end illegal commerce between villagers and foreign pirates. For 150 years Monte Cristi lay abandoned until it was resettled by farmers from the Canary Islands.

The Victorian buildings lining the streets reflect the town's European influence and include a large French clock dating from 1895 in the Parque Central.

Right: unearthed at La Isabela

THE SAMANÁ PENINSULA

Dense forests of palm trees shading a carpet covered with bromeliads and orchids clothe the gentle green hills; little vegetable gardens frame brightly painted cottages; waterfalls plunge through lush tropical vegetation. On the Samaná Peninsula lie lonely beaches of sand as fine and white as caster sugar, where the sea is warm and as blue as a picture postcard. Here, seeing the world through rose-coloured glasses does not require the assistance of a rum cocktail.

Cayo Levantado

It has to be said that nowadays this exceptionally beautiful island only lives up to the desert island idyll early in the morning or late at night: it's not easy to find a quiet corner between the stalls of shellfish and fizzy drinks, and the lobster-coloured visitors.

Las Galeras

Recently mass tourism has made its appearance in Las Galeras with the development of an all-inclusive resort. And yet the town is still the perfect setting for successfully doing nothing at all.

For the more active visitor there is diving, or from Moby's Whale Watch Restaurant on the precipitous cliffs you can watch the huge marine mammals through binoculars without getting too close.

El Limón

Most people reach El Limón waterfall from Las Terrenas on what is effectively a mule train, led by a Dominican guide. The ride on mules or horses takes about one hour, crossing alarmingly steep hills, bridle paths and muddy cattle tracks. The water plunges over 40 metres (130 ft) into a pool that provides an inviting opportunity to cool off. Depending on the season and the weather conditions, the ground may prove to be quite slippery, making the ride correspondingly adventurous.

Punta Bonita

The road west out of Las Terrenas is currently in a lamentable state. But it is worthwhile enduring the 5 km (3 miles) of bumps and ruts to get to Punta Bonita, the perfect destination for those in search of complete peace and the opportunity to do nothing more than relax beneath the palm trees.

Santa Bárbara de Samaná

For years, yachts from all the corners of the world have dropped anchor in Santa Bárbara de Samaná, the provincial capital, overlooked by the port that clings to the shore between two hills. There

Left: view over Samaná bay **Right:** *the beach at Las Terrenas*

are plans to redevelop the area to accommodate a harbour for cruise ships and a marina with berths for 600 yachts. To reach Santa Bárbara de Samaná travellers can drive through the hills, or take a ferry ride across the Bahía de Samaná from Sabana de la Mar, which affords the most attractive view of the little port as it chugs into the harbour. However, the ferry is for foot passengers only.

THE CIBAO VALLEY

Rice, bananas, tobacco, cocoa and coffee all prosper here, and lorries, heavily laden with sugar cane or oranges, thunder along the busy *autopista*. The region in the north of the island is the *República*'s bread basket: between Santiago, La Vega and Salcedo a thick layer of black fertile soil covers the ground. Rainfall is heavy in the southeastern section of the valley, which runs for 200 km (125 miles) between the mountain ranges of the Cordillera Central and the Cordillera Septentrional. That there is no shortage of water is due also to the rivers Yaque del Norte and Yuna.

Above: Dominican gold at the Bermúdez Rumfabrik

Santiago de los Caballeros

Santiago de los Caballeros is one of the most important cities in the country, a fact which it owes to the Autopista Duarte, giving it a direct link to Santo Domingo 155 km (96 miles) away to the south. It is an important economic and business centre, and also the second largest metropolis in the land.

BERMÚDEZ RUMFABRIK

The northwestern district of Santiago de los Caballeros is where most people go to taste the *República*'s pride and joy for themselves and see how it is made. The Bermúdez Rumfabrik rum distillery is a long building on the Avenida J. Armando Bermúdez on the corner of Blanca Mascaro.

CATEDRAL DE SANTIAGO APÓSTOL

In the centre of the little Parque Duarte is a small pavilion, behind which rises the Catedral de Santiago Apóstol, built between 1868 and 1895 in a style that combines classical and neo-Gothic elements. Inside is an elaborately carved mahogany altar, decorated with gold leaf, and the beautiful stained-glass windows *(vitrales)* were completed by the artist José Rincón-Mora during the 1980s.

MONUMENT TO THE HEROES OF THE WAR OF RESTORATION

The city's most prominent landmark is the Monumento a los Héroes de la

Right: Catedral de Santiago Apóstol

Restauración de la República. It is 67 metres (220 ft) tall and was erected by order of President Rafael Leonidas Trujillo in honour of the heroes of the War of Restoration. In the entrance hall you can inspect the murals by the artist Vela Zanetti; his work also adorns the United Nations Building in New York. The top of the column, surmounted by an allegorical female figure, can be reached via a staircase, and there are wonderful views over the city.

MUSEO DEL TABACO

The exhibits in the Museo del Tabaco provide a wealth of information about the tobacco plant – all the more interesting because the tobacco industry is one of the most important economic factors of the Cibao Valley region. The exhibits, photographs and text are arranged in an illuminating manner throughout the museum, and an English guide is available.

Salcedo

The town of Salcedo witnessed a bloody chapter in the nation's history. A small metal monument at the entrance to the town, and the portraits of the *Tres Hermanas Mirabal* painted on the wall

Above: Monumento a los Héroes de la Restauración de la República

recall the fact that the three Mirabal sisters: Patria, Minerva and María Teresa – like many other political opponents and thousands of Haitians – were murdered by the henchmen of the dictatorial President Trujillo in November 1960. In the Plazoleta de las Hermanas Mirabal, a small square near the village of Ojos de Aguaon, lies the frame of the car in which the outspoken sisters died and a 5-metre (16-ft) sculpture dedicated to their memory. The little Museo de las Hermanas Mirabal is 5 km (3 miles) beyond Salcedo on the way to San Francisco de Macorís.

Santo Cerro

The Santo Cerro, or "Sacred Hill", can be found about 10 km (6 miles) north of La Vega and it is here that a legend, dating from the time of the conquista-dors, was born. The story goes that in 1495, under the leadership of the cacique Guarionex, the Taínos went into battle against the Spanish. When they attempted to burn the cross which Columbus had erected, the Virgen de las Mercedes suddenly

appeared and protected the Christian symbol from the flames. As a result, the Amerindians were persuaded to accept its authority. Whether you believe the story or not, the place is worth a visit because from behind the church there is a magnificent view of the valley, the forests of palms and the amapola trees, which are a wonderful sight in February when they are covered in coral-red blossom.

Right: the Tres Hermanas Mirabal *are honoured in Salcedo*

La Vega

Also known as La Concepción de la Vega, La Vega is a quiet provincial town. The historic buildings that are still standing – the Palacio de Justicia, the Teatro La Progresista and the fire station, the Bombería – all date from the beginning of the 20th century, when the railway line to Sánchez created an economic boom for the town. The most recent architectural addition is the Nueva Catedral (1992). It is a building full of pomp and circumstance in which the Biblical number 12 is of great significance: 12 doorways lead into the interior, and 12 round windows provide light.

February is the best month to visit the town, as then all hell is let loose every Sunday. Dominicans all agree that the pre-Lenten carnival in La Vega is the most magnificent in the land. *Diablos cojuelos* ("Limping Devils") in garish costumes dance through the streets, their faces hidden behind gruesome masks. They take great delight in attacking bystanders with pigs' bladders filled with water.

CORDILLERA CENTRAL

The "Dominican Alps" are a magnet to nature lovers, with beautiful alpine flora, clear mountain air and stunning panoramas of the surrounding rolling landscape. Hence the central region's attraction to active sports enthusiasts who flock to the area to hike, cycle and horseback ride through the picturesque countryside or to visit the national parks with their complex ecosystems and unique vegetation. The mountain peaks offer cool relief from the heat inland and on the coast and have the highest elevations in the entire Caribbean.

Above: a typical La Vega carnival mask

Constanza

The town in one of the highest valleys in the country at 1,200 metres (3,940 ft) above sea level has a temperate climate although the mercury does drop below zero degrees Centigrade in winter. Here the combination of a mild climate and fertile farmland produces abundant crops of fruit and vegetables (mainly garlic and strawberries) not usually grown in the Caribbean, and also beautiful flowers for export.

Jarabacoa

This small town in a lush valley 528 metres (1,732 ft) above sea level on the eastern bank of the Río Yaque del Norte is a rich agricultural and farming area producing fruits and vegetables as well as a wide variety of flowers. The valley is irrigated by the Río Yaque del Norte, the country's longest waterway and an ideal place for rafting. There are several ranches in the area which offer water rafting tours and other action-packed

Above: the Cordillera Central is green and lush

activities such as tubing, canyoning, hiking and excursions through the countryside on horseback or in jeeps to El Salto de Baiguate and El Salto de Jimenoa outside Jarabacoa.

Parque Nacional Armando Bermúdez

One of the Republic's large national parks is the Parque Nacional Armando Bermúdez with its steep ground covered by native pine trees. The climate is alpine with cool weather, the temperature

dropping below freezing point during the winter months. In December and January the mercury can reach –8°C (18°F) during the night, and the rising sun reveals frost-covered bushes and vegetation, creating a type of ghostly scenery that is unexpected in the Caribbean.

There are a number of well-trodden hiking trails leading through the park, up to the mountains and Pico Duarte. Most of the trails start at one of the many ranger stations in the valley. Among the wildlife that populates the area are a rich variety of birds such as the cotorra, a small parrot indigenous to Hispaniola; the woodpecker; the cigua palmera (palm chat), the national bird; the

Above: rural Jarabacoa

papagayo; and the Guaraguao, a rapacious bird that preys particularly on small rodents.

Parque Nacional José del Carmen Ramírez

South of Parque Nacional Armando Bermúdez and west of Constanza is Parque Nacional José del Carmen Ramírez.

Together the two national parks are home to more than ten of the Dominican Republic's main river systems and therefore have the most plentiful water resources in the country. The national park is also home to the source of the Río Yaque del Sur.

Pico Duarte

The highest elevation in the Antilles' is Pico Duarte, which at 3,087 metres (10,128 ft) towers above the central region's two main national parks, Parque Nacional Armando Bermúdez and Parque Nacional José del Carmen Ramírez, which lie in the foothills of the mountain. Neighbouring peaks are La Pelona (3,080 metres/10,105 ft) and La Rucilla (3,045 metres/9,990 ft).

No one attempted to climb Pico Duarte until 1944, but today there are several trails leading to it. During his term as president, the dictator Trujillo christened the mountain Pico Trujillo, but with his fall the imperious peak was renamed after the founding father and 19th-century revolutionary Pablo Duarte. The best time to climb is between March and October.

Right: *hanging heliconia*

AROUND LAGO ENRIQUILLO

Here the island shows its more frugal and varied side. The road cuts through a desert-like landscape reminding even the most unpoetic of a surreal Dalí painting. Moody as the hot and arid west can be, lush rainforests appear, at the feet of gigantic *sierras* (mountain ranges), along with deserted pebble beaches, the world's second-largest salt lake, and two national parks where Amerindian caves and petroglyphs are reminders of the islands early inhabitants.

Azua de Compostela

This bustling city nowadays lives off its flourishing agriculture. The town was founded in 1504 17 km (11 miles) to the north by the Spanish soldier Diego Velásquez (1465–1524), who later con-

quered and governed Cuba. Yet the shipping metropolis, once home to the conqueror of Mexico, Hernán Cortés, regularly suffered heavy pirate attacks. Eventually, in 1791, Azua was wiped out by an earthquake, and the town was rebuilt on its present site. Several times, Azua was burned to the ground until the gory battle of 19 March 1844 brought the Dominicans independence from Haiti. The battle, which is honoured by a monument in the Parque Central, took place at Puerto Viejo, where you can still see some colonial ruins, and where the great Taíno leader Enriquillo is said to be buried.

Above: bustling Azua de Compostela

Bahía de las Aguilas

The region's best beaches, scattered with large conch shells, are in the Bahía de las Aguilas, a little-known hot-spot for scuba divers and snorkellers, which can only be reached in a four-wheel-drive or by boat.

Baní

Dubbed the "city of poets", Baní means abundance of water. Founded by immigrants from the Canary Islands in the 18th century, the town is friendly. Except for the Museo de Máximo Gómez, which honours the native 19th-century Cuban liberation fighter, there is not much to see, although coffee junkies should check out the Museo del Café Dominicano where the Dominican wonder bean is documented. Great pictures can be taken at the lively Mercado Modelo near Parque Central. The city beach, Playa Baní, is hard to reach, but definitely worth the bumpy ride.

Above: *a distinctive cemetery in Baní*

Barahona

The last big town in the southwestern part of the *República* is Barahona, 80 km (50 miles) from Azua. It's hard to imagine this provincial port town ever being an El Dorado for the all-inclusive set, or as the "Boca Chica of the Southwest". It is only a matter of time before this untouched part of the island disappears under a sea of development, but for the moment there are only a few neat hotels catering to tourists. The airport is actually named for Barahona-born Hollywood actress, Maria Montez. She made more than 20 films during the 1940s, including *The Arabian Nights* and *Ali Baba and the Forty Thieves*.

The real attraction of the town is its position at the top of the Península de Pedernales giving easy access to the beautiful national parks. Driving high up into the Alp-like mountains of the Sierra de Baoruco affords views of magnificent scenery, and south from Barahona is "the Côte d'Azur of the Dominican Republic".

Above: *colourful Barahona fire station*

Lago Enriquillo

The extremely dry landscape surrounding Lago Enriquillo distinguishes the Dominican Republic from most of the other islands in the Greater Antilles. Almost every corner holds some historical value, since the legendary chieftain Enriquillo hid from the Spaniards with his men in the rocky mountains of the adjacent Sierra de Baoruco and Sierra de Neiba, waging war against them for over 14 years. In 1533, on Isla Cabritos in the middle of Lago Enriquillo, he signed the first peace treaty between the Taínos and the colonials with an envoy of the Spanish king. The treaty guaranteed his people a reservation and himself the honorary title of "Don".

If you get an early start from Barahona (6am is perfect), you can make the tour around Lago Enriquillo in eight hours.

Parque Nacional de Isla Cabritos

Walk through the shady tropical forest of the Parque Nacional de Isla Cabritos, which is home to iguanas that are larger than domestic cats, to reach the boats that cross over to Isla Cabritos (Goat Island). But don't expect to see goats once you arrive there. Instead, the 12-km (8-mile) long island is home to some of the rarest animals in the Caribbean: crocodiles, rhinoceros iguanas and ricord iguanas, large turtles and 62 species of birds, including flamingos, Hispaniolan parrots and spoonbills.

Right: Lago Enriquillo's dry landscape

Reserva Antropológica de las Cuevas de Borbón

North of Caoba is the Reserva Antropológica de las Cuevas de Borbón. This is a series of 40 interconnecting caves, which include the Cuevas de El Pomier, where there are more than 5,000 petroglyphs and several thousand Amerindian wall paintings. The caves are also home to thousands of bats (don't forget the flashlight).

Las Salinas Peninsula

About 30 km (19 miles) southwest of Baní, the salt gardens of the Las Salinas Peninsula jut into the sea, and the area has

been protected as a National Monument. The bleach-white salt hills have a surreal note, with the windy Bahía de Las Calderas to the right and the panoramic Sierra Martín García behind. For a pleasant swim in a beautiful setting, take the road north to Palmar de Ocoa. This quaint fishing village has a neat grey beach and weekend *haciendas* for affluent city folk.

San Cristóbal

Standing on the banks of the Río Nigua like a mini version of bustling Santo Domingo is San Cristóbal. The industrial capital of the southwest is notorious as the birthplace of

***Above:** a heron among the mangroves, Las Salinas Peninsula*

Rafael Leonidas Trujillo y Molina, who left numerous landmarks around town. It is hectic and polluted, and not very friendly towards tourists. Recognising the first Constitution of the Dominican Republic, which was signed in the early 19th century after a rebellion against the Haitians in the local Palacio del Ayuntamiento (city hall), the dictator officially named San Cristóbal the "Meritorious City". However, today there is not much of meritorious value left here, and its sights will take only about two hours to visit.

Close to the Parque Duarte stands the neoclassical church of Nuestra Señora de Consolación where you can see Trujillo's tomb. The corrupt Trujillo spent a fortune on his home town, building the church in 1946 at an astronomical cost of US$4 million from government funds, along with the renovated plaza in front where, ironically, the city cannot afford to provide the fountains with water.

Above: *the church of Nuestra Señora de Consolación, San Cristóbal*

ESSENTIAL INFORMATION

The Place

The Dominican Republic shares the island of Hispaniola with the Republic of Haiti. It has almost 1,600 km (1,000 miles) of coastline and is bordered to the north by the Atlantic Ocean and the Caribbean Sea in the south.

Population: 8 million.

Language: Spanish.

Religion: Apostolic and Roman Catholic.

Time Zone: Eastern Standard Time (GMT –5 hours). Daylight Saving applies during summer.

Currency: the peso; but US dollars are widely accepted.

Weights and Measures: the decimal metric system should be used. However, pounds and ounces are used in weighing solids and cooking oil, fabrics are measured in yards, and petrol (gasoline) and motor oils are measured by the imperial gallon (128 oz). On the other hand, rum, beer and other liquids are sold in bottles of 0.756 litre. Land surfaces in urban areas are measured by square metres and in rural areas they are generally measured by "tarea" (1 tarea = 624 sq. metres).

Electricity: 110–120 volts, 60 cycles.

International Dialling Code: 809

The Climate

The average temperature in the Dominican Republic is 25°C (77°F) year-round. The climate on the coasts is more tropical than in the central part of the country, where temperatures are cooler. The average amount of rainfall varies depending on where

Left: relaxing on the beach at Juan Dolio

you are in the country. On the northern coast the rainy season falls in Oct–April/May and in the south it is from May–Oct/Nov. The northern and eastern towns have the most rain.

The Economy

Four major industries sustain the Dominican Republic's economy: agriculture, mining, tourism and duty-free zones. In recent years tourism and duty-free zones have been the most dynamic money-earners. Presently, tourism provides the greatest economic gain to the country, followed by duty-free zones in which textiles, electronic equipment, cigars, etc are produced for export.

The main exports in the agricultural sector are coffee, cacao, sugar, pineapples, oranges, plantains, bananas, vegetables and flowers. The Cibao Valley region is not only rich in agricultural products but is also home to large deposits of ferronickel and the largest open-air gold mine on the continent, La Rosario Dominicana. Other mined exports are gypsum, marble and rock salt.

Above: refreshments available by the beach

Public Holidays

New Year's Day (January 1); Day of Our Lady of Altagracia (January 21); Independence Day (February 27); Good Friday (March or April); Easter (March or April); Corpus Christi (May or June); Day of Our Lady of Mercedes (September 24); Christmas Day (December 25).

The following holidays are observed on the closest Monday to these fixed dates: Epiphany (January 6); Juan Pablo Duarte's birthday (January 26); Labour Day (May 1); Dominican Restoration Day (August 16); Constitution Day (November 6).

Getting There

BY AIR

Direct scheduled or charter flights from Europe depart from airports in London, Madrid, Rome, Lisbon, Amsterdam, Bonn, Düsseldorf, Stuttgart, Brussels, Frankfurt, Helsinki and Paris, among others.

US routes link the Republic with Toronto, Montreal, Ottawa, Quebec City, Halifax, Dallas, Minneapolis, Boston, Newark, New York and Detroit. There are also direct flights from Latin American cities including Caracas, Panama City, La Paz, Santiago de Chile, Buenos Aires, Bogata and Cancun. Over 60 charter airlines fly to the international airports of Puerto Plata, Punta Cana and Santo Domingo.

Right: get around by gua-gua bus

BY SEA

There are cargo and passenger shipping services operating from New York, New Orleans, Miami and South American countries. Several cruise lines from the US, Canada and Europe include the Dominican Republic on their itineraries. You can obtain details from the Republic's tourist offices in the country concerned.

Entry Regulations

A visa is not required to enter the Dominican Republic for citizens of the United States, Canada, Spain, France, UK, Germany, Switzerland, Italy, Venezuela, Scandinavian countries, Panama, Uruguay, Costa Rica, Japan, Dominica, Brazil, Argentina, Antigua, Bermuda, the Netherlands Antilles, Guade-

loupe, Martinique, Jamaica, Mexico or Trinidad and Tobago. Citizens of these countries only require a US$10 tourist card, and proof of citizenship (passport, original birth certificate, etc.). Visitors from all other countries need an entry visa.

Health

The Dominican Republic is a safe destination provided you take the proper precautions. The vaccinations recommended to all visitors to the tropical Caribbean islands are Hepatitis A and Hepatitis B.

Tap water is not safe to drink on the

Above: *female family members*

island. Visitors should drink bottled water or purified water, which is available everywhere. For people travelling to major hotels and resorts, there are clinics available on the premises. Otherwise, local hospitals and clinics will treat independent travellers. In any case, make sure you have adequate health insurance.

Money

The Dominican monetary unit is the peso (RD$). Coins are 1, 5, 10, 25 and 50 cents and 1 peso, and bills are in denominations of 5, 10, 20, 50, 100, 500, and 1000 pesos. You will receive more for your dollars or pounds if you exchange them at a commercial bank upon your arrival in the country. By law, banks are required to place a slate in public view stating the exchange rate for the day. Most hotels, restaurants and commercial establishments accept major credit cards and they are legally bound to use the correct exchange rate on them. US dollars are also widely accepted.

Above: old stamps are worth many pesos

Security and Crime

In an emergency, dial 911. This 24-hour number will connect you with the police, Red Cross, fire service, civil defence and emergency centres.

The Dominican Republic is one of the safest destinations in the Caribbean. However, it is important to be cautious. Do not carry large amounts of money; do not leave valuables unattended at any time and avoid walking along unlit streets after dark. The Department of Tourism has a special security force called the *Politur* or *Policia Turistica* (Tourist Police). Officers provide information and guidance to visitors on security matters.

Tipping

In addition to an 8 percent tax, restaurants add a 10 percent service charge to all bills, which is passed on to employees. If you receive exceptional service it is appropriate to give an extra tip.

Useful Addresses

Department of Tourism: Secretaria de Estado de Turismo, Avenida México, tel: 1-809 221 4660, 1-200-3500 (toll-free in the Dominican Republic), fax: 1-809 682 3806. Puerto Plata, tel: 1-809 586 3676; 18–22 Hand Court, London WC1V 6JF,

Above: report any crime to the police

United Kingdom, tel: 020 7242 7778, fax: 020 7405 4202.

National Park Administration: Dirección Nacional de Parques, Avenida Máximo Gómez, Cementerio Antiguo, Santo Domingo, tel: 1-809 472 4204, fax: 1-809 472 4012.

Ecotourism: Ecoturisa, Santo Domingo, tel: 1-809 221 4104, fax: 1-809 685 1544.

Foundation for the Investigation and Conservation of Marine Life: Fundacion Dominicana por Investigacion y Conservacion de los Recursos Marinos: Avenida Anacoana 77, Santo Domingo, tel: 1-809 686 3250.

Useful Websites

The following websites provide general information in English:

● *www.hispaniola.com* for events, restaurants and shopping.

● *www.dr1.com* for news and useful tourist information.

● *www.thedominicanrepublic.net* for business and tourist advice.

Disabled Travellers

The Dominican Republic is not yet fully equipped to accommodate disabled travellers, but it is possible to find hotels that meet the needs of travellers with specific needs. Consult your travel agent, or one of the following organisations that specialise in advising disabled travellers:

● Access to Travel Magazine Inc., PO Box 43, Delmar, NY 12054 1105, USA, tel: 518 439 4146; fax: 518 439 9004.

Right: Bayahibe beach babe

● Royal Association For Disability and Rehabilitation (RADAR), 12 City Forum, 250 City Road, London EC1V 8AF, UK, tel: 020 7250 3222; fax: 020 7250 0212; Minicom: 020 7250 4119; Email: radar@radar.org.uk

Women Travellers

Women travelling alone can move around relatively safely in the Dominican Republic. Use the same common sense that you would in any city or unfamiliar place. Stick to populated areas by day and night. And don't be too surprised if local men blatantly attempt to charm you.

Travelling with Children

Most larger hotels and resort complexes offer facilities and a range of entertainment activities for children, as well as the services of trained child minders.

Tropical Weddings

Getting married in the Dominican Republic is becoming increasingly popular with couples who want to combine the ceremony itself with the honeymoon, and bring friends and family along too. Whether you want to tie the knot on a picture-postcard beach or in a pretty Caribbean chapel, most tour operators, hotels and

Above: youngsters can have fun in the Republic

resorts offer all-inclusive pack-
ages. Some hotels have dedicated
wedding planners who can organ-
ise packages that include an
indoor or outdoor ceremony, the
services of a civil judge, a wedding cake, champagne and flowers. Other services include music,
photography and video. Before
the ceremony the couple must ful-
fil a three-day residential require-
ment and provide official documents translated into Spanish.

Carnival and Festivals

February is Mardi Gras time, one of the oldest traditions of the
island. Each region has its own carnival and the season concludes
with a colourful parade down Avenida George Washington
(known as the Malécon) in Santo Domingo. Festivities in La
Vega are considered to be the best but there are also carnivals
in Santiago and Monte Cristi.

The famous two-week Merengue Festival which takes place
in July in Santo Domingo along the Malécon, is a lively fun event
that attracts crowds of Dominicans from all over the country,
along with foreign visitors. In October Puerto Plata is the venue
for the north's own Merengue Festival and cultural events.

Tours and Excursions

In the Dominican Republic, all of the all-inclusive resorts are
affiliated with tour operators who offer their specialist tours to

Above: choose a mask and join the carnival

visitors. If you are travelling independently there are many tour companies to choose from, no matter which part of the country you are staying in. A few of the better-known operators include: **Colonial City Tours**, tel: 687 5245, which organises tours around the Zona Colonial and Santo Domingo, with commentary in English, Spanish or French; **Get Wet** in Puerto Plata, tel/fax: 586 1170 arranges river raft trips, canyoning, caving and cascading down waterfalls; **Iguana Mama** in Cabarete, tel: 571 0908 has excursions to Pico Duarte, horse riding, mountain bike tours, scuba diving and specialist family trips.

Las Cascades

There are adventure trips by jeep through the sugar cane fields of Imbert to Las Cascades with its caves and eight-level waterfall. You can dive, climb or swim in the refreshing clear waters.

Samaná–Cayo Levantado

In the northeast, you can drive through the countryside to the white-sanded bay of Samaná. The waters around Samaná Bay are a whale sanctuary and every winter (Dec–Mar) humpback whales mate close to shore. Once in Samaná, head to the Fisherman's Marina for a motorboat trip to Cayo Levantado (Barcardi Island). Contact Victoria Marine, tel: 538 2588.

Above: a boat tour around Laguna Gri Gri *Right:* capital shoeshine

SANTO DOMINGO CITY TOUR

Cultural highlights of the capital city are the Palacio Nacional, Faro a Colón and the Zona Colonial, including the Panteón Nacional.

WATER RAFTING

Raft through the rapids and canyons of the Río Yaque del Norte and see some mountain scenery in the Cordillera Central that's only accessible from the river.

PLAYA GRANDE AND LAGUNA GRI-GRI

A trip to the Costa Verde, Río San Juan, where you can take a ride in a motor launch through the crystal clear waters of Laguna Gri-Gri, featuring mangroves and bird life.

Language

The official language of the Dominican Republic is Spanish. Most people at the tourist resorts speak some English, but it is useful, and appreciated, to know a few key words and phrases.

USEFUL PHRASES

Yes *si* (see)

No *no*

Please *por favor* (por fa-vor)

Thank you *gracias* (grass-ee-ass)

Excuse me/sorry *perdone* (pair-don-ay)

Please speak slowly *por favor hable despacio* (por fa-vor a-blay des-pasio)

Do you speak English? *habla usted inglés?* (a-bla oo-sted ing-lays)

I don't understand *no entiendo* (no en-t-en-do)

Hello/hi! *hola* (oh-la)

Good day/morning *buenos días* (b-wen-os dee-os)

Good night/evening *buenos noches* (b-wen-os noch-es)

Goodbye *adios* (a-dee-os)

See you later *hasta luego* (as-ta lu-way-go)

How are you? (singular) *cómo está?* (com-o es-ta)

Okay/fine *muy bien* (m-wee bee-en)

Bill (check), please *La cuenta por favor*

How much? *Cuanto cuesta?*

You're welcome *De nada*

Can I see a room? *Puedo (Podemos) ver un cuarto?*

What is the rate? *Cual es el precio?*

A single room *Un cuarto sencillo*

A double room *Un cuarto doble*

Key *llave*

Bathroom *Reterete, lavabo*

Left: strolling in Sosúa

And now for the big picture...

The text you have been reading is extracted from *Insight Guide: Dominican Republic & Haiti*, one of more than 200 titles in the award-winning Insight Guides series. Its 390 pages are packed with expert essays covering the island's history and culture, detailed itineraries, comprehensive listings, a full set of cross-referenced maps, and hundreds of great photographs. It's an inspiring background read, an invaluable on-the-spot companion, and a superb souvenir of a visit. Available from all good bookshops.

Also from Insight Guides...

Insight Guides is the award-winning classic series that provides the complete picture of a destination, with expert and informative text and the world's best photography. Each book has everything you need, being an ideal travel planner, a reliable on-the-spot guide, and a superb souvenir of a trip. Nearly 200 titles.

Insight Maps are designed to complement the guidebooks. They provide full, clear mapping of major destinations, list top sights, and their laminated finish makes them durable and easy to fold. More than 100 titles.

Insight Compact Guides are handy reference books, modestly priced but comprehensive. Text, pictures and maps are all cross-referenced, making them ideal books for on-the-spot use. 120 titles.

Insight Pocket Guides pioneered the concept of the authors as "local hosts" who provide personal recommendations, just as they would give honest advice to a friend. Pull-out map included. 120 titles.

☆ INSIGHT GUIDES

The world's largest collection of visual travel guides